20 Questions: Earth Science

What Do You Know About Weather and Climate?

PowerKiDS press
New York

Gillian Gosman

Published in 2014 by The Rosen Publishing Group, Inc.
29 East 21st Street, New York, NY 10010

Copyright © 2014 by The Rosen Publishing Group, Inc.

All rights reserved. No part of this book may be reproduced in any form without permission in writing from the publisher, except by a reviewer.

First Edition

Editor: Jennifer Way
Book Design: Kate Laczynski
Layout Design: Colleen Bialecki

Photo Credits: Cover Lyle Leduc/Workbook Stock/Getty Images; p. 5 MaszaS/Shutterstock.com; p. 6 PhotoLink/Photodisc/Getty Images; p. 7 Brand X Pictures/Thinkstock.com; p. 8 Matthew Cole/Shutterstock.com; p. 9 Rehan Qureshi/Shutterstock.com; p. 10 Johan Swanepoel/Shutterstock.com; pp. 11, 12 iStockphoto/Thinkstock.com; p. 13 Ozerov Alexander/Shutterstock.com; p. 14 Comstock/Thinkstock.com; p. 15 (top) Todd Shoemake/Shutterstock.com; p. 15 (bottom) Vladislav Gurfinkle/Shutterstock.com; p. 17 Peter Kunasz/Shutterstock.com; p. 18 z576/Shutterstock.com; p. 19 Tony Campbell/Shutterstock.com; p. 20 Artiomp/Shutterstock.com; p. 21 Hemera/Thinkstock.com; p. 22 Zoonar/Thinkstock.com.

Gosman, Gillian.
 What do you know about weather and climate? / by Gillian Gosman. — 1st ed.
     p. cm. — (20 questions: Earth science)
 Includes index.
 ISBN 978-1-4488-9701-8 (library binding) — ISBN 978-1-4488-9860-2 (pbk.) — ISBN 978-1-4488-9861-9 (6-pack)
 1. Weather—Miscellanea—Juvenile literature. 2. Climatology—Miscellanea—Juvenile literature. I. Title.
 QC981.3.G67 2013
 551.6—dc23

2012032070

Manufactured in the United States of America

CPSIA Compliance Information: Batch #S13PK5: For Further Information contact Rosen Publishing, New York, New York at 1-800-237-9932

Contents

What Do You Know About Weather and Climate? 4
1. What is weather? 6
2. What do scientists who study weather measure? 7
3. What causes the seasons to change? 8
4. Why is there more daylight in the summer? 9
5. What is the Sun's role in weather? 10
6. Why does warm air rise? 10
7. What causes wind? 11
8. How do clouds form? 12
9. What is precipitation? 12
10. What causes different kinds of precipitation to form? 13
11. What causes thunderstorms? 14
12. What causes tornadoes? 14
13. What causes tropical storms and hurricanes? 15
14. How do landforms affect weather? 16
15. How is climate different from weather? 16
16. What is climate change? 18
17. What causes changes in the climate? 19
18. What is the greenhouse effect? 20
19. What human actions cause climate change? 21
20. What are people doing about climate change? 22
Glossary 23
Index 24
Websites 24

What Do You Know About Weather and Climate?

You see different weather when you step outside every day. Some days it is sunny, while other days might be windy, rainy, or snowy. Weather is a worldwide system of powerful forces. Changes in the weather are caused by many things, such as the heat of the Sun, the movement of water across oceans, and the weight of the entire **atmosphere** that surrounds Earth.

In this book, we will explore what drives these forces and how they come together. We will look at the tools scientists use to measure and forecast the weather and at how weather and climate have changed during Earth's history.

Did you ever wonder why it snows only when it is cold? This book will explain what causes snow and other forms of weather.

1. What is weather?

Weather is the condition of the atmosphere in a particular place on a particular day. For example, it might be sunny and warm in one town while it is windy and cloudy in a nearby town.

This meteorologist is looking at pictures sent from a satellite to observe how weather is moving through an area.

2. What do scientists who study weather measure?

THERMOMETER

Meteorologists are scientists who study the weather using many different tools. They measure air temperature using thermometers. They use **barometers** to measure **air pressure**. They measure how much precipitation falls and how much water vapor is in the air. They measure wind speed and wind direction. They use **satellites** and **radar** to see weather patterns. These tools all help meteorologists forecast the weather.

3. What causes the seasons to change?

The four seasons are based on Earth's position in relation to the Sun as Earth **orbits** on its **axis** around the Sun. Both the angle and the strength of the sunlight that Earth receives changes throughout the year because Earth's axis is tilted. These changes are what cause Earth to have different seasons.

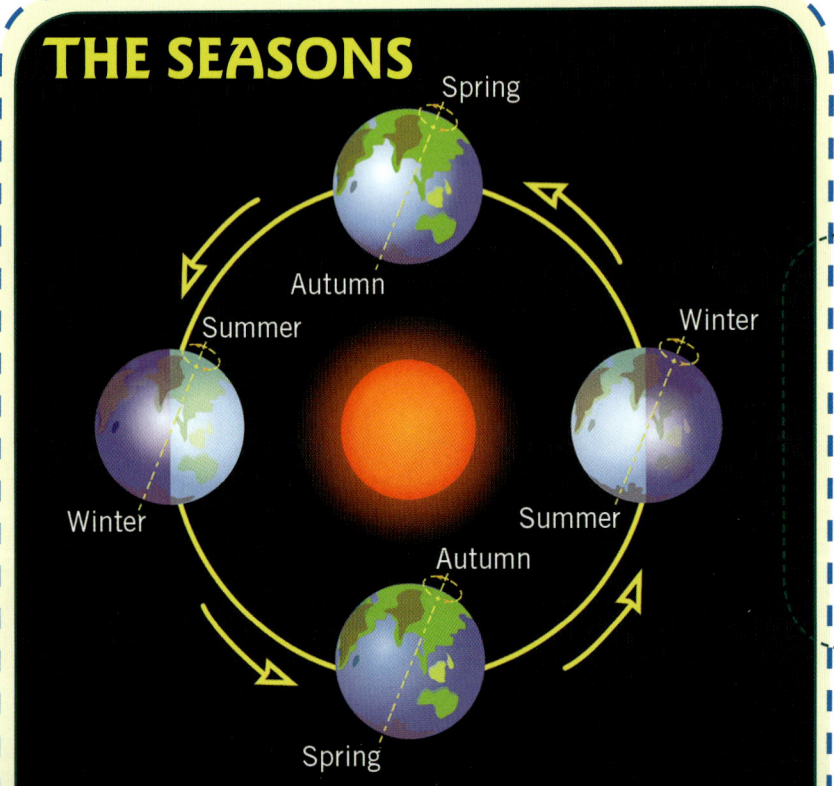

This diagram shows how Earth moves on its axis around the Sun over the course of the year. Earth's axis is shown as a dotted line.

Many people like to eat ice cream on hot summer days.

4. Why is there more daylight in the summer?

During the summer there are more hours of sunlight and that sunlight is hitting Earth at a more direct angle. This is why summer is warmer than winter. The Northern Hemisphere and the Southern Hemisphere are tipped toward the Sun at different times of year. This means that the seasons on each hemisphere are the opposite of one another.

5. What is the Sun's role in weather?

The Sun is a driving force behind weather. One of the most important things it does is warm Earth's surface. Weather is created in part because the Sun warms Earth's surface unevenly.

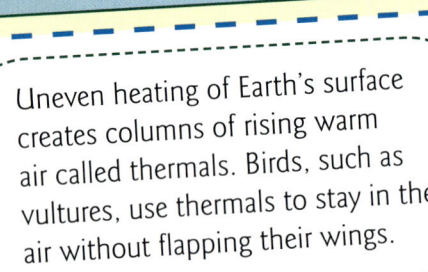

Uneven heating of Earth's surface creates columns of rising warm air called thermals. Birds, such as vultures, use thermals to stay in the air without flapping their wings.

6. Why does warm air rise?

Heat moves from where it is warm to where it is cooler. Warm air has lower air pressure, or force pushing down on it, than cool air. This causes warm air to flow upward. As the air flows upward, it cools and becomes denser, meaning it has more air pressure. This cooled air then falls.

7. What causes wind?

Wind is the movement of warm air rising and cool air falling. The greater the temperature differences between the warm air and cool air, the greater the difference in air pressure and the stronger the wind.

The air is always moving, and sometimes this creates very strong winds!

8. How do clouds form?

Clouds form as part of the **water cycle**. This is the process of the Sun **evaporating** water, the water vapor **condensing** and forming clouds, and then water falling as precipitation.

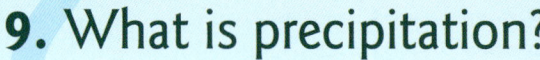
CLOUDS

9. What is precipitation?

Precipitation is any water that falls to the ground from clouds, no matter in which form it falls.

The ground must be below 32° F (0° C) for snow to stick to it. Otherwise the snow will melt as it lands.

10. What causes different kinds of precipitation to form?

When the air temperature is above 32° F (0° C), precipitation falls as rain. Water freezes below this temperature, which is how snow, freezing rain, sleet, and hail form. Freezing rain is rain that hits cold air and freezes as it falls. Sleet is a mix of rain and snow. Hail is balls of ice that form in very cold parts of storm clouds and are sometimes seen during thunderstorms.

LIGHTNING

11. What causes thunderstorms?

Thunderstorms form when **static electricity** builds within clouds. This causes a spark of electricity called lightning to jump between two clouds or between a cloud and the ground. The lightning causes a quick change in air temperature and air pressure, which causes thunder.

12. What causes tornadoes?

A tornado can form when a thunderstorm contains unusually warm air near the ground and unusually cold air higher in the atmosphere. Then the wind must begin to blow in different directions and at different speeds at different heights in the storm, forming a funnel cloud.

TORNADO

13. What causes tropical storms and hurricanes?

Tropical storms and hurricanes form over tropical oceans. As ocean water evaporates, large amounts of water vapor make the air very humid, or wet. High winds then spin the air into a tropical storm. If the storm grows large enough, it becomes a hurricane.

Hurricanes, like the one shown in this satellite picture, bring not only strong winds but also lots of rain.

14. How do landforms affect weather?

Landforms, such as hills, mountains, and canyons, play an important role in weather. Consider a mountain. As wind moves across Earth's surface, air is forced up one side of a mountain. This is called the windward side of the mountain. As the air rises, it cools and condenses, forming clouds. The clouds are often trapped on the windward side, and this side of the mountain gets most of the precipitation. The other side of the mountain, called the leeward side, tends to have calmer and drier weather.

The western, windward sides of the Rocky Mountains tend to have pine forests. The leeward sides tend to have drier grassland areas.

15. How is climate different from weather?

Weather is the condition of a place from day to day. Climate is the average weather condition of a place over very long periods of time.

16. What is climate change?

Climate change is the change in Earth's weather patterns over time. Earth's climate has changed throughout its four billion years. For example, there have been ice ages, or periods during which ice sheets covered much of Earth's land. Climate change has a huge effect on life on Earth.

Ice sheets are found near Earth's North Pole and South Pole. This ice has frozen and melted as Earth's climate has changed over time.

17. What causes changes in the climate?

A drought is a long period of time without rain. Droughts are caused by changes in an area's normal weather pattern.

Some things that cause climate change are natural, including the movement of continents over many centuries. Volcanic eruptions and changes in ocean currents can cause climate change, too. In the past 50 years, scientists have been studying how human activities, such as burning **fossil fuels**, cause changes to Earth's climate.

18. What is the greenhouse effect?

The greenhouse effect is the process in which the Sun's heat is held in and bounced back into space by gases in Earth's atmosphere. In this way, the atmosphere acts as a blanket, keeping Earth warm. Human activities, such as burning fossil fuels, release extra greenhouse gases into the atmosphere. The rise in greenhouse gases is causing Earth as a whole to become warmer.

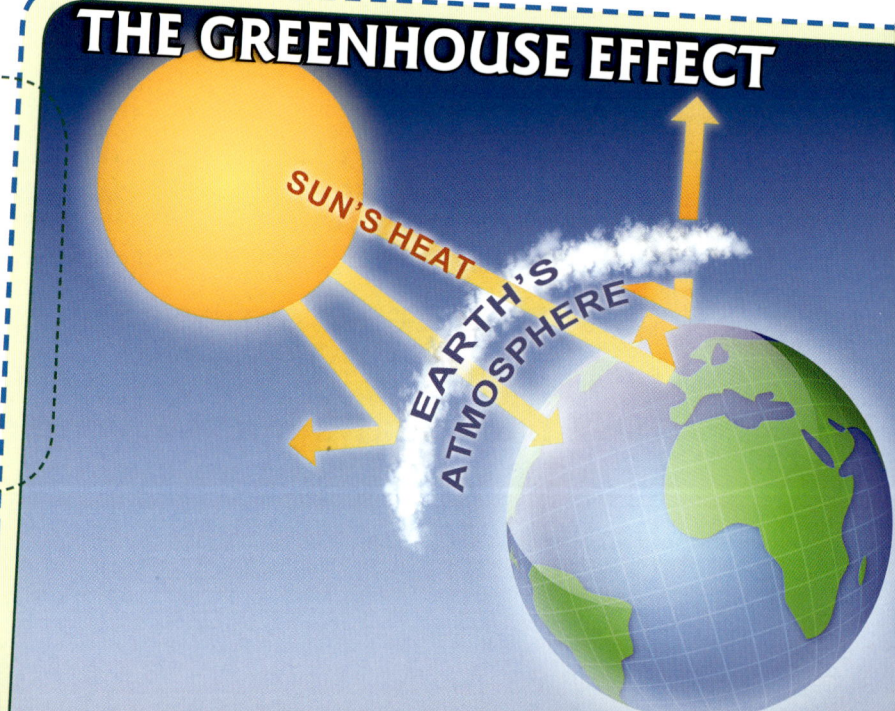

This diagram shows how the greenhouse effect works. The greenhouse gases in Earth's atmosphere hold in some of the Sun's heat to warm the planet. Some of the heat gets bounced back into space.

19. What human actions cause climate change?

Factories that burn fossil fuels, like coal, let out greenhouse gases. Adding extra greenhouse gases to Earth's atmosphere is believed to cause climate change.

Scientists who study Earth's climate have noted that changes in Earth's climate have become more frequent and more powerful. They believe that these changes are caused by the warming of Earth brought about by the rise in greenhouse gases. This means that human activities are likely causing changes to Earth's climate.

20. What are people doing about climate change?

We can do things to lessen the effects of climate change caused by human activities. We can lower the amount of greenhouse gases we release into the atmosphere by lowering our use of fossil fuels. Fossil fuels such as gasoline run most cars, and oil and coal are burned to create the electricity we use in our homes.

We can also increase our use of energy sources such as solar energy and wind energy. These energy sources create electricity without releasing greenhouse gases. We can also plant more trees, which help absorb some greenhouse gases. This is something simple you can do to help Earth's atmosphere.

Wind farms, like the one shown here, turn the power of the wind into electricity. These work best in places where it is usually very windy, though!

Glossary

air pressure (EHR PREH-shur) The weight of the air.

atmosphere (AT-muh-sfeer) The gases around an object in space. On Earth this is air.

axis (AK-sus) A straight line on which an object turns or seems to turn.

barometers (buh-RAH-meh-turz) Tools used to measure air pressure, or the weight of air.

condensing (kun-DENTS-ing) Cooling and changing from a gas to a liquid.

evaporating (ih-VA-puh-rayt-ing) Changing from a liquid, like water, to a gas, like steam.

fossil fuels (FO-sul FYOOLZ) Fuels, such as coal, natural gas, or gasoline, that were made from plants that died millions of years ago.

meteorologists (mee-tee-uh-RAH-luh-jists) People who study the weather.

orbits (OR-bits) Travels in a circular path.

radar (RAY-dahr) A machine that is used to predict weather.

satellites (SA-tih-lyts) Machines in space that circle Earth and that are used to track weather.

static electricity (STA-tik ih-lek-TRIH-suh-tee) Electricity in which the electrons creating the electricity move very little.

water cycle (WAH-ter SY-kul) The natural process of water drying up and forming clouds then falling back to Earth as rain.

Index

A
air pressure, 7, 10–11, 14
atmosphere, 4, 6, 14, 20, 22

C
change(s), 4, 8, 14, 18–19, 21–22
condition, 6, 16

E
Earth, 4, 8–9, 18, 20–21

F
force(s), 4, 10

H
heat, 4, 10, 20

M
meteorologists, 7

O
oceans, 4, 15

P
process, 12, 20

R
radar, 7

S
satellites, 7
seasons, 8–9
Sun, 4, 8–10, 12
system, 4

T
temperature, 7, 13–14
thermometers, 7
tools, 4, 7

Websites

Due to the changing nature of Internet links, PowerKids Press has developed an online list of websites related to the subject of this book. This site is updated regularly. Please use this link to access the list: www.powerkidslinks.com/20es/weath/